Quality living without being cruelly frugal :
80 proven tips
Peter K. Black

Copyright © 2014 Pierre Jereczek

All rights reserved

To my readers and my wonderful wife

Table of Contents

The truth about frugality.

Lifesaving tips for quality sustainable living.

Tip #1:

Tip #2:

Tip #3:

Tip #4:

Tip #5:

Tip #6:

Tip #7:

Tip #8:

Tip #9:

Tip #10:

Tip #11:

Tip #12:

Tip #13:

Tip #14:

Tip #15:

Tip #16:

Tip #17:

Tip #18:

Tip #19:

Tip #20:

Tip #21:

Tip #22:

Tip #23:

Tip #24:

Tip #25:

Tip #26:

Tip #27:

Tip #28:

Tip #29:

Tip #30:

Tip #31:

Tip #32:

Tip #33:

Tip #34:

Tip #35:

Tip #36:

Tip #37:

Tip #38:

Tip #39:

Tip #40:

Tip #41:

Tip #42:

Tip #43:

Tip #44:

Tip #45:

Tip #46:

Tip #47:

Tip #48:

Tip #49:

Tip #50:

Tip #51:

Tip #52:

Tip #53:

Tip #54:

Tip #55:

Tip #56:

Tip #57:

Tip #58:

Tip #59:

Tip #60:

Tip #61:

Tip #62:

Tip #63:

Tip #64:

Tip #65:

Tip #66:

Tip #67:

Tip #68:

Tip #69:

Tip #70:

Tip #71:

Tip #72:

Tip #73:

Tip #74:

Tip #75:

Tip #76:

Tip #77:

Tip #78:

Tip #79:

Tip #80:

CONCLUSION:

THE TRUTH ABOUT FRUGALITY.

Frugality to many is something so difficult and almost impossible to do and entails a lot of odd things to incorporate. But unlike its misnomer and often associated with to being a cheapskate. Frugality is about sensible living. But still, even in extreme frugality there are options to take. One is to cut back on everything in a sensible way and live happily for the rest of your life or you can go live in laxity which is impossible to maintain and live miserable in the end. It's a choice against good and evil, against good and bad. Some people try so hard and deny themselves too much almost certain that they end up disappointed with their chosen lifestyle.

One way to live with frugality is to seek alternatives to find and buy less expensive items or stop unnecessary habits and expenses trying not to do things that will deprive you with quality and make you feel inferior or cheaply value less.

Many people view food such as grocery items as the first thing to cut down on spending. While it is true that there are many options to save money on food items, one must never forget that the quality and nutritional merits of the food you are going to eat or feed to your family. If the choice is between prepared and ready to go food from the restaurant and fast food chains and a home cooked meal prepared with the food items from your grocery list. It is value wise to choose the latter. Not only because those items in your grocery list were carefully thought has that best suited your nutritional need and that of your family. Since you specifically have specifically have chosen them during your shopping whereas those fast food and restaurant food items are chosen for general consumption not specifically for you. This is the sense of why we do food shopping. It is not mastering about frugality that matters but instead how a person becomes sensible enough to deal with life's rough ends. Choosing the best at less the price and having several options to go further does matters most. You don't need to have everything. Having enough to sustain a well-nourished body and mind is wealth to last a lifetime. To choose the best value for us and our family. This is the sense in what frugality is all about. The same philosophy that works on all the other areas and aspects of wise buying and spending.

Lifesaving tips for quality sustainable living.

Using time, effort and resources combined with spending and living wisely will not only result in improved productivity and efficiency but improved economic. Our everyday lives are full of struggles and trivialities that most of us sometimes cannot deal at once. But living with these practical life values will not only help you guide your everyday living but greatly help in motivating you in all life dealings. As we move on an continue facing and bracing for all these life struggles, we can also see that there are options and choices that can become and produce positive results that affect us, our family and extend to our other circles and community. As we practice and execute these lifesaving tips and guides, the feeling of being at our best overflowing with positivism and optimism tends to radiate and ripples down to the people around us and gets back up to us in overwhelming results bringing us comfort and ease as we experience quality living.

Attaining life sustainability comes in many forms. But attaining quality sustainable living must be done with matters of sensible motivation combined with hard work, determination, focus and discipline. The rewards of life comes swiftly if you always act with life challenges accordingly. A person's quality of life depends on how he works for and consume his share of the pie. For many people, their version of what the 'good life' normally involved luck, hard work and focusing on increasing material wealth and at the same time attain social economic stature in the shortest time possible. They simply neglect one important factor in pursuing to brand their lives truly rewarding. They often forgot that in attaining the 'good life' there must be 'value' to make it worthwhile. Most people through their lifetime amass wealth and money thinking it would give them anything and everything. Sadly, most of these people tend to catch up with time and in the end realizes that the money they have cannot buy back the time they lost to return to scenes where they needed to put values and worth and find themselves too late to reverse back and correct those unnecessary habits and things that made them miserable in the end. They forgot to act on life accordingly thus in the end life has acted upon them. If you don't like how your life is going, you always have the option to change how things are. Remember that our body in time will take the tolls of all our activities. And most find themselves busy trying everything to change for the better. If you stumble and don't know how to drive your life for the better, consider the following simple and practical guides for the better.

Tip #1:

Delegate. Remember that 2 heads are better than one. You might have a grand plan but executing it needed more minds to it. Assigning task will definitely solve the trivialities of a job and will aid in the early accomplishment of it.

Tip #2:

Prioritize according to ease. Cue doing jobs according to your ease and expertise. This way you can do a multitude while trying to do last those that you have uncertainty or taking much time and effort to do.

Tip #3:

Organize your everyday 'to do' list. Making this a habit will keep you updated of what your daily milestones has to be within the day. As you review and organize, you might discover some are not anymore necessary and can be omitted upgrading your daily tasks.

Tip #4:

Schedule tasks accordingly. The practical way to do scheduling is to its urgency and significance. Once you have scheduled the task, accomplish each one according to your pace and interest. This way you shall have accomplished most that inspire you leaving those tough and difficult to deal with later.

Tip #5:

Spend procrastination wisely. Let every time spent productively and make the short idleness the only leisure time you can afford as you continue with each and every task.

Tip #6:

Set deadlines. Give a time frame to each task and utilize time around it. If you cannot accomplish it yourself, find remedy by delegating or seeking help to do such.

Tip #7:

Start early. As they say: The early bird catches the early train. Starting early offers that opportunity to get the job done right, early and on time.

Tip #8:

Work with your favorites. Everybody has a favorite. Favorite shirt, favorite, food, favorite chair, favorite pen, etc. Start working with what inspired you best. The inspiration will go a long, long way. The feeling good mood on working using your favorite things could offer productivity sometimes even beyond expectations.

TIP #9:

A sticky note is always a handy tool. Writing a note especially to someone while the person is out in a post-it note is a wise idea saving you less effort on communication to a person. Can likewise save you money if you are saving your phone battery or electronic load money instead of calling the person. Bookmarking using sticky notes on important chapters and notes of a book while you're in transit can save you time of browsing and revisiting what you have been reading.

TIP #10:

Keep a time diary. Maintaining one whether manual or virtual offers like you have an extended memory bank within your reach.

TIP #11:

Just say 'Yes or No' and never 'Maybe.' It always pay to be honest. If you can't make the task for whatever reason it maybe will help you make a stand right now. Whatever reason may come later if you feel not telling it. The most important thing is you cut short and address immediately the situation, allowing time to define a task and stop you from changing minds and be fickle with your decision. An unsure reply will just take more time and can sometimes cost money.

Tip #12:

Seek help. Rely on your own skills wholeheartedly but there is nothing wrong if the option for help is around. It gets the task done in less time altogether.

Tip #13:

Learn a free app. Google Docs, Trello, Sunrise Calendar and Cloudmagic are just some of the hundreds of free apps that are quite handy and value added to increase productivity on your everyday tasks.

Tip #14:

Challenge yourself and maintain your email. To add more challenge to your email routine task, some apps are developed to make it more challenging and improve productivity. Do the email game. The email game is an efficiency app to whiz you off your full email inbox and act on each at the quickest possible time with each function given an equivalent points value to accomplish as rewards.

Tip #15:

Start your own Do it yourself (DIY) bank. Why not? You need not be a banker to start your own home made depository. You can save those change and coins by dropping them on a piggy bank, a penny bank, a coin jar a coin pocket or a cash box. Once its full and heavy, that's your cue to crack and open it and deposit it to the bank where it will earn further interest.

Tip #16:

Save for a purpose. The purpose of saving is to do something with the money. Saving money is wonderful when you have a goal in mind. But saving just to save can cost you your happiness.

Tip #17:

Be a DIY person. Why pay the price of having things done for yourself when you can do it by yourself. It will not only save you money but improve your self-sustainability skills. Be a handyman and learn to fix things like a real life fixer/handyman.

Tip #18:

Learn how to sew and repair your own clothes. Instead of buying new set of clothes in lieu of a damaged one, why not repair the damage if it's just a simple damage that can easily be sewn.

Tip #19:

Buy neutral colored clothes. Neutral colored pieces can be easily mixed-match to suit your everyday attire.

Tip #20:

Use hand me downs. Wearing the old shirt of your brother and your shoes from a dear friend may look great on you anyway than buying new clothes you'll only wear for a short period of time.

Tip #21:

Use clothesline instead of dryer. Drying clothes naturally on clothesline saves you drying electricity using your machine.

Tip #22:

Make your own cleaning solutions. Those toxic and hazardous ingredients in your cleaning solutions can pose health hazards. Why not make your own cleaning solutions using baking soda, vinegar, lemon and soap. They are not only environment friendly but even cost you less or nothing at all.

Tip #23:

Set aside a maintenance day. Maintenance day is the day a person set aside to do everything that relates to weekly housekeeping like laundry, grocery shopping, house or room cleaning, lawn mowing, gardening, etc. You can group these tasks in a day for you to focus more time on high level tasks the rest of the week.

Tip #24:

Be a couponer. Those coupons are treasures and money. So don't waste them. Hunting and saving up those coupons and redeeming them while shopping not only can give you discounts and freebies they actually are goodwill money sponsored by food and service providers in exchange for your continued patronage of their products or services.

Tip #25:

Buy in bulk. If you have necessities that you consume in large quantity, buying in bulk will be best and practical, saving you effort, time and money frequenting the stores just buying them.

Tip #26:

Grab on groupons. Deals for the day are basically offered everywhere on anything. They are up for grabs for a limited time so grab them good before they're gone.

TIP #27:

Utilize cash or money back credit card schemes. They were great grabs from the card company. Considering you have that money back security if you bought a defective or unusable one.

TIP #28:

'No money' strip tag. Post a 'you have no money strip tag' on your wallet to motivate remind and restrain you from pulling cash from your wallet.

TIP #29:

Master the 30-day replenishment cycle. Condition your mind that what you have bought today will last for 30 days and the next time you're going to have that opportunity to buy it again is until next month.

Tip #30:

Buy for value not with price. Though most things comes with a price for their value. Buying things with should always have a purpose. If you can afford a choice, always choose value over price.

Tip #31:

Bust impulse buying by practicing the 10-second rule. The 10-second rule is a shopper's practice where one got to ask oneself within 10 seconds a valid reason why to buy an item before putting it inside the shopping cart. If there is no valid reason to buy, the item must be returned to its shelf and continue to shop without the overruled item.

Tip #32:

Drink free water. When you're in a restaurant and gets thirsty, request for a free glass of water instead of ordering soda or expensive beverages.

Tip #33:

Stick to your shopping list. Create and bring a shopping list when buying things and never put anything in your cart if it's not on the list.

Tip #34:

Eat less red meat. Red meat is not the only source of protein. Combining your vegetarian meals with egg, yogurt, cheese and milk offer a complete and balanced diet.

Tip #35:

Go vegetarian. A vegetarian diet of vegetables, fruits, beans, soy and grains are less expensive even with the cheapest cuts of meat. A practical way to do this was to gradually do it. Initially by eating less meat or eating fruits and vegetables one full week in a month until you got used to it. There are foods to substantiate protein from meat, thus you still can achieve full nutrition and nutrients nourishing without meat on your diet.

Tip #36:

Eat fruits and vegetables in season. You will not only have the chance to have lots of choices and variety, you will also enjoy lesser prices for in season food produce are cheaper by its season.

Tip #37:

Say no to junk. Completely cut off these unhealthy food. If you do, you will not only have a healthy body but a healthy wallet as well.

Tip #38:

Give up liquor, alcohol and smoking. It is not only great for your health but healthy also on your budget.

Tip #39:

Exercise regularly and avoid stress. Exercise pumps up production of the endorphins in our brain achieving and attaining our satiety and feel good neurotransmitters keeping us feeling good and motivated.

Tip #40:

Say no to social events that are not necessary. Of course you still need to socialize. It's all part of being human and living with people anyway but learn how to say no to some of it and limit your attendance on those urgently important and greatly needed attention like your own family events.

Tip #41:

Avoid eating out. Dining out costs more than home cooked meals and could definitely ruin your budget before you knew it.

Tip #42:

Cut on sugars. Sugary food will only tend to make you eat more and could lead to unhealthy conditions like obesity and heart diseases.

Tip #43:

Eat leftovers. Don't let it go to waste and your money wasted. Leftovers can still be eaten and reheated to regain crisp and freshness.

Tip #44:

Read eBooks. Instead of buying or renting books, eBooks are around to fill in on your leisure readings. There are practically thousands of book materials online that can save you huge money buying them on paper or hardbound. You also save money going around on bookstores and libraries just to read them.

Tip #45:

Use LED lights. Replace light bulbs with LED lights. They are more economical than ordinary incandescent or fluorescent lights. LED only uses 2% that of incandescent bulbs consumption. LED might cost a bit higher but will last longer and efficiently.

Tip #46:

Use crayons for emergency lighting. In an emergency, use a crayon for light. Remember crayons are made with wax. It can still burn for the next 30 minutes. Just be careful to place it in a secure container and place in a safe place away from combustible materials.

Tip #47:

Observe everyday earth hour and turn off the lights. By turning off unnecessary lights, you can do your share in reducing the global warming phenomenon.

Tip #48:

Use water filters. Instead of buying bottled water, consider installing and using water filter and drink water from the faucet. Will not only save you money on buying bottled water but you will also reduce the waste throwing away those empty water bottle.

Tip #49:

Use pail and dipper in your toilet and showers. Using them instead of the shower and toilet bowl flush can save you gallons and gallons of water and money to pay water bills.

Tip #50:

Grow your own garden. Home garden technology using aquaponics or drip irrigation systems are popular choices. With the age of science and technology, growing a garden need not need that much ground space.

Tip #51:

Consider public transport when travelling within the city. If accessible, consider travelling using the city's public transport. It will not only save you on gas, car maintenance and parking. It will also be a good way to see the city using another medium of transportation.

Tip #52:

Carpool. Share and participate to conserve gas and help ease traffic congestion.

Tip #53:

Shop on bargains and thrift shops. It will not only help you save hundreds of dollars. Sometimes, the style and fashion is not that off and could fit you great.

Tip #54:

Insulate water heaters during winter and fall. This will help keep the warmth saving you money on heating.

Tip #55:

Install solar panels for energy. Sunlight is free and harnessing its power for our everyday electrical energy is not only practical but a great way to achieve minimal to zero electric bill.

Tip #56:

Practice the 3Rs of conservation. Reduce, reuse, and recycle. As an act of goodwill to Mother Nature, everyone is being encouraged to reduce waste and waste materials, reuse things to conserve life and longevity of everything we are using and recycle to give back to earth what we have taken and use.

Tip #57:

Consider cheap quality crafts for gifts. There are a number of online sites offering quality handmade crafts at amazingly low prices and great gift ideas.

Tip #58:

Try to practice a 'no spend' day. Motivation comes easy if you have the will and desire to do it. Living a day in your life without spending a cent will not only earn you great rewards financially but will also break that habit on impulsive buying.

Tip #59:

Use generic prescriptions instead of branded medicines. They only differ in packaging but the efficacy are but just the same.

Tip #60:

Use programmable thermostat on appliances. Save energy by using a programmable thermostat in operating appliances like air conditioning units, heaters, etc. The device will help you manage usage of your appliances according to when you only wanted your appliances to start operating.

Tip #61:

Try buying and using refurbished. Consider using refurbished items rather than buying brand new especially for single or temporary use.

Tip #62:

Use online bills payment. This will save you the time and effort going to business centers just to pay your bills. You will also have the opportunity to check on your bank balances as it updates.

Tip #63:

Always practice that 'Never give up.' mentality. Financial struggles are being experienced by all not only you. Millions worldwide are trying to cope with their everyday lives and many have emerged victorious and successful going through and have even made doing saving and productivity ideas their way of life. Applying and sharing life lessons to everyone and free their minds with financial worries.

Tip #64:

Your computer is all you need. Instead of buying TV and radio just to watch TV shows or tune in to your favorite radio show, you can have both with just your computer and internet.

Tip #65:

Go paperless. Before printing a page, think first if you really need a hard copy printed. You might consider just saving an image copy for your file copy. Imagine saving on paper and ink as well as electricity if you can just save it on your file for your reference.

TIP #66:

Utilize electronic battery energy. Consider using the reserve power of your electronic gadgets, laptops, cell phones, cameras etc. The reserve power in the batteries of your electronic gadgets could save you electrical consumption.

TIP #67:

Shop online. Consider shopping online. It will not only save you time and effort but money on gas and other savings.

TIP #68:

Reusable grocery bags. When doing grocery shopping, use reusable grocery bags instead of plastic or paper bags. You will not only maximize using it but will help in eco waste conservation.

TIP #69:

Baking at night. You will not only conserve energy while using the oven when temperature is cool but you will also warm up the house and fill it with yummy decent and goodies.

TIP #70:

Rubber band on paint can. Tie a rubber band across the opening of paint can to scrape off excess paint on the paint brush. This will save and utilize much the content paint in the can.

TIP #71:

Home phone vs. cell phones & internet phones. Weigh on choosing the fitting communication phone. The facilities of internet communication via websites and apps like Skype and other media could be bundled as to your preference. If you use internet that often and you communicate much using it, you might want to discontinue using your home phone and use internet phone communication instead. Should you need mobile communication you certainly have the choice between cell phones and internet communication as well.

TIP #72:

Watch movies on the internet. Want to have a moonlighting date with your dearie? Why not spread a blanket in your grassy lawn? Set up your wifi and laptop, pop some popcorns, set up a bonfire and skew some hotdogs on stick. Enjoy movie watching while moonlighting.

Tip #73:

Subscribe on online news and magazines. Cut off deliveries of your dailies and subscribe online where you can read them anywhere, anytime. This will also reduce those unnecessary clutters and piles in your house and help in managing and maintaining order in the house.

Tip #74:

Shop after the holidays. The best drop down sales happen after the holidays where commercial centers are redressing big discounts and slashing off big to fish shoppers on low selling days.

Tip #75:

Discover new road routes. This will not only help you save time on discovering short cuts on your way to work, school, etc. It will also pave way to cut gas and car maintenance consumption.

Tip #76:

Sell your garbage. Learn how to segregate the items in your bins. Bottles, plastics, old appliances and metal have corresponding value in your community junk dealer. You will not only cash in on your junk, you will also contribute in the world's move in proper disposal of garbage and wastes.

TIP #77:

Pay in cash and stop using your credit cards. Minimize charges to your spending by using cash and not your credit card. Some credit cards charge add ons on top of their service and interest fees to accommodate your credit spending. Using cash will be more advantageous in terms of bank charges and fees.

TIP #78:

Set a price limit to your buying. Before going to a store, set in your mind as to how much you are going to spend or bargain on every item. Say, if you're buying a pair of shoes. Peg it at $100 if it goes beyond that amount, forget buying it and save your money on your next shopping schedule. This practice will also limit your urge to go beyond your budget and stick to it.

TIP #79:

Go biking instead of going to the gym. Biking could make your body fit and trim as effective as going to the gym. Biking works on all your body muscles and joints and is a very good calisthenics exercise for the body.

Tip #80:

Unplug. Take off and unplug all electrical cords in the outlet. Plugged electronics even when off continue to draw power even if you are not using them. Just leaving them plugged on electrical sockets still consume electricity and may cause unwanted electrical accidents especially during power surges and can cause further damage to your electronics.

CONCLUSION:

Frugality is life's new addiction to sensible living.

Some people have been practicing frugality all their life all in an attempt to find ways to live and survive through the challenges life brings. But through the many ways on how to practice frugality many had found out that there is no one single way that fits everyone. This is mainly because all of us are unique individuals with diverse needs and wants. But one good thing that counts is that the sense that frugality brings to everyone were being creatively done in a number of ways with many people benefiting from it moving economic mountains and portals. The quest for sustainability in this ever diversified world is taking into higher levels and being optimized by many to benefit and gain from it more. Gone are the days when frugal people are being criticized and mocked because of the odd ways they live and save up through their lifetime. Today, frugality has become a habit, passion and lifestyle to many who wanted to achieve more in life and be successful in every task they do. Frugality is the new fancy and addiction to sensible living.

www.ingramcontent.com/pod-product-compliance
Lightning Source LLC
Chambersburg PA
CBHW070729180526
45167CB00004B/1677

In today's world, many of us are living looking for ways to reduce expenses, effort and time while still enjoying quality life with value and worth. While it is possible to live a quality life, one need not be cruelly frugal in every way just to sustain quality living.

You can save money, manage your time efficiently and still be productive yet doing things on a much practical way. Enjoy healthy and delicious food with less spendings and costs. Dress and look classy and dignified without spending much on designer and signature apparels.

Work and give each task and activity utmost planning and time management for a more efficient and productive living. These are the basics within a person's motivation for quality living in the most practical sense without going to the limits of everyday living.